THIS BOOK BELONGS TO

Still ME!

_____

WHAT'S WRONG WITH THAT DOG?

(THAT CAT'S REBUTTAL TO: "WHAT'S WRONG WITH THAT CAT?")

By

JAMES CORNELIUS CRAWFORD, M.Ed.

who is this guy?

What's wrong with that dog? A cat's rebuttal.

To order additional copies please write to the publisher at
the address below.

RAY HAK BOOKS
An imprint of:
DIAMOND AND HALO PUBLISHING, LLC
PO BOX 20091
Cincinnati, Ohio 45220

DIAMOND AND HALO PUBLISHING, LLC

ISBN 978-1-~~955181~~

For
Rayya Sabreen
and
Hakeem Omar:

My beloved children,
who still love books.
And for all children
who love books.

I love books, too!

Shut up.

He's always digging up the yard,
And leaving all these holes,
What the heck is he looking for?
No one really knows.

But if *I* do something wrong,
I'm accused of being bad,
If I dig just *one* hole,
Everybody gets mad!

WHAT IS THAT?

It's a hole—like the one in your head.

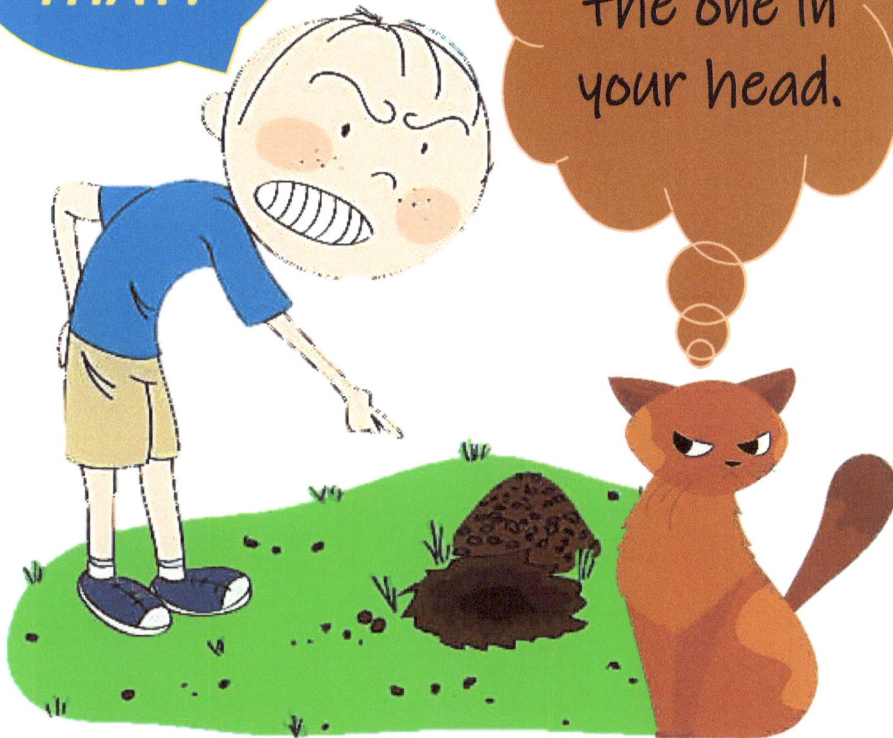

Where ever that dog poops,
You gladly pick it up,

When *I* have an "accident",
You turn orange and start throwing up!

You wanna get that?

Stupid dog howls at the moon,
Even when it's not in sight,

Howl!

But let me meow just *once*,
And you put me out at night.

Meow?

GET
OUT!

When *I* do-do on the floor,
You kick me out of the place,
But the dog eats his own poop,
And then licks you in the *face*!

He even licks your feet,
And you don't seem to care,

That dog licks *everything*,
And he licks *everywhere*!

What the...?

So, the dumb dog likes to kiss—
I *don't*.

Don't try to force me, because—
I *won't*!

Give me a ki—
OUCH!

"NO" means "NO".

That dumb dog chases his tail,
And when he catches it,

He stands there looking stupid,
Asking, "What do I do with it?"

He even chases *cars*,
And whenever he can,

He chases that poor old
Frightened letter-man.

I run all over this place
Chasing that stupid old mouse,

And while I sleep in a *box*,
That dumb dog has his own *house*!

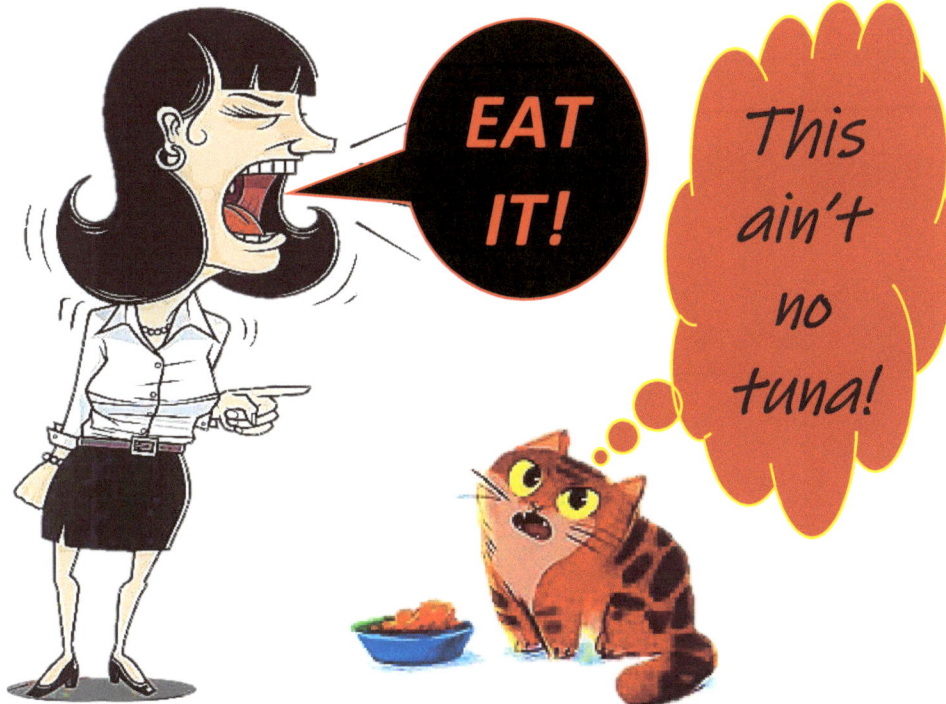

He comes to your dinner table,
And just stands there and begs,

That dog drinks toilet water
When he's not humping your legs.

Whenever he comes from outside
That dog tracks mud everywhere,
But you never say a word
When he muddies up your chair.

That dog just tears up the place
Whenever he comes through the door,

You say nothing, but have a fit
When I put one scratch on the floor.

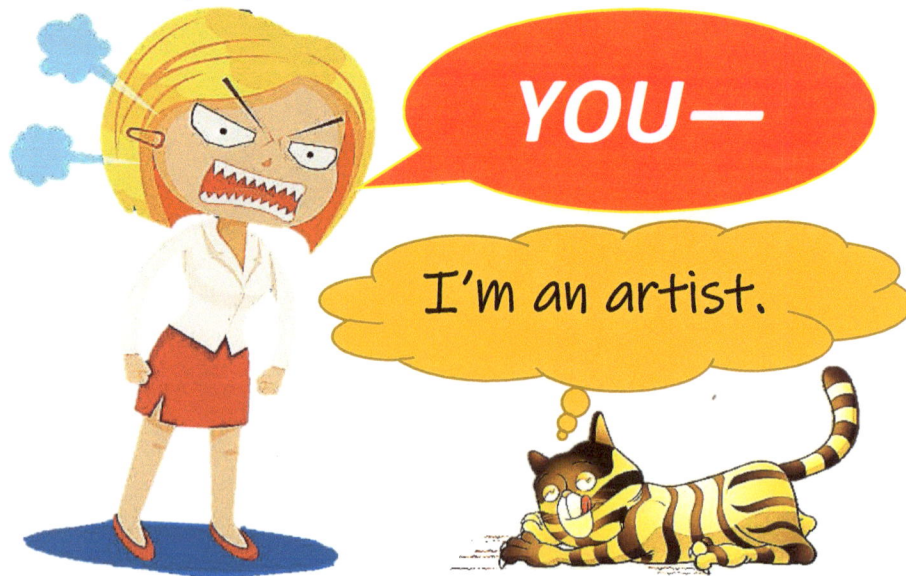

YOU—

I'm an artist.

That dog is *always* barking,
He barks at his own *shadow*,
But it gets worse than that—
He barks at the *rain* and *snow*.

That dog barks at *everything*,
Even if nothing is there,
That mutt is so stupid that
He even barks at the air.

I tell the kids good bye
When they go off to school,

GOOD Bye, KITTY!

Get lost.

But that dog chases their school bus
Like some mangy flea-bag fool.

One day that mangy mutt
Came chasing after me,
I watched him for two hours
Barking up the wrong tree.

That dog bothers everyone,
And never does what he's told,

Down, boy!
No! Stop!
Sit! Heel!

I *never* talk to strangers,
Cats are never that bold.

Come here, kitty!

I don't know you.

That dog just brings you garbage,
Like stinky bones and old hats,

But I bring you better gifts,
Like plump and juicey *rats*.

What?
It's dead.

The mutt can come back home when
He's done howling with his friend,

But when I go sing with *my*
Cats, I have to *sneak* back in.

That dog needs to be petted,
To be walked and thrown a bone;

But I don't need none of that,
Just leave me the *heck* alone!

Nice kit—

Don't touch me.

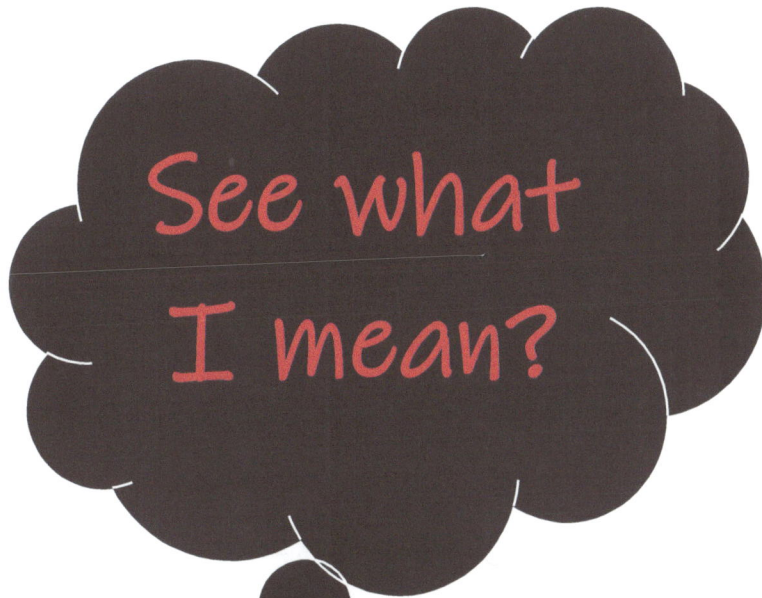

ABOUT THE AUTHOR

James Cornelius Crawford

James is a lover of cats *and* dogs, but sometimes cats get a bad rap, and they (cats) believe that dogs get away with all kinds of stuff.

These are just a few "episodes" that cats witness every day in regards to how tolerant pet owners are to their dogs compared to their cats.

Maybe they got a point? They seem to think so.

James is a former Early Childhood Educator (Though what teacher isn't *ALWAYS* a teacher?), with two undergraduate degrees in Early Childhood Studies, and Early Childhood Care and Education from the University of Cincinnati, and a Masters of Education Degree, concentration in Special Education, from Xavier University.